Contents

What makes Earth special?

Earth is the only place in the solar system where there are living things. Plants, animals and people need air, water and warmth. Earth has all of these. That makes it special.

WOW!

Scientists think there are more than eight million different types of living things on Earth!

Our Solar System

EARTH

Mary-Jane Wilkins
Consultant: Giles Sparrow, FRAS

Published in paperback in 2017 by Wayland

© 2017 Brown Bear Books Ltd

Wayland
An imprint of Hachette Children's Group
Part of Hodder & Stoughton
Carmelite House
50 Victoria Embankment
London EC4Y 0DZ
An Hachette UK Company
www.hachette.co.uk
www.hachettechildrens.co.uk

ISBN 978 1 5363 0284 7

Brown Bear Books Ltd
First Floor, 9–17 St. Albans Place
London N1 0NX

Author: Mary-Jane Wilkins
Consultant: Giles Sparrow, Fellow of the Royal
Astronomical Society
Picture Researcher: Clare Newman
Illustrations: Supriya Sahai
Designer: Melissa Roskell
Design Manager: Keith Davis
Editorial Director: Lindsey Lowe
Children's Publisher: Anne O'Daly

Printed in Malaysia

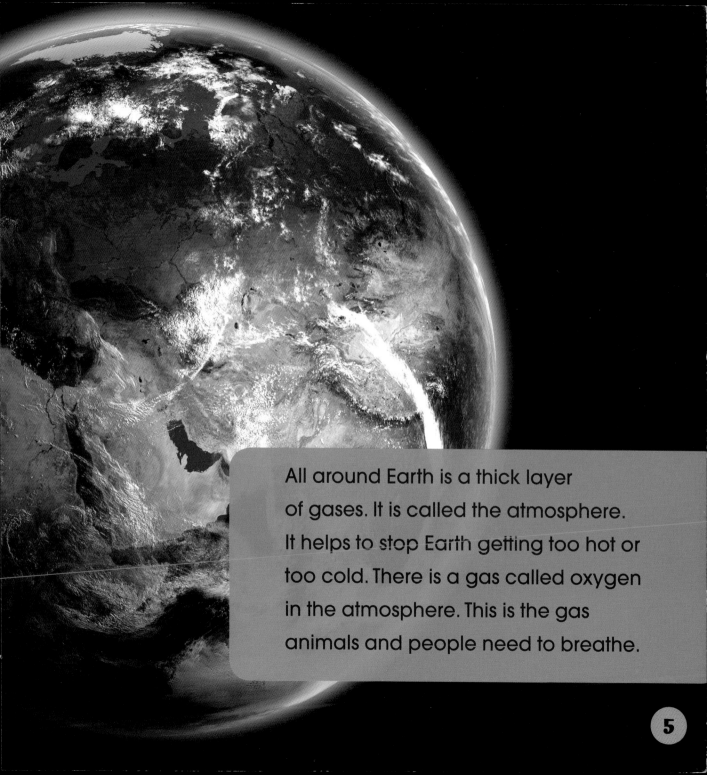

All around Earth is a thick layer
of gases. It is called the atmosphere.
It helps to stop Earth getting too hot or
too cold. There is a gas called oxygen
in the atmosphere. This is the gas
animals and people need to breathe.

Earth in the solar system

Earth is a planet that travels around, or orbits, the Sun. The Sun is a star. It is a huge, shining ball that sends out the heat and light we call sunshine. Without the Sun, Earth would be a dark and cold place.

Mar

Jupiter

Comets fly around in space, too. These lumps of rock and ice look like giant snowballs.

Mercury

Venus

Earth

Earth's Moon

Seven other planets orbit the Sun. They are Mercury, Venus, Mars, Jupiter, Saturn, Uranus and Neptune. Dwarf planets go around the Sun, too. Pluto is a dwarf planet. The Sun, the planets and other space objects make up the solar system.

Uranus

Neptune

Pluto (dwarf planet)

Saturn

Watery planet

Most of Earth is covered with water.
There is water in the oceans, lakes
and rivers. There is frozen water, too.
In very cold places, such as the North
and South Poles, water is frozen as ice.

Earth is
sometimes called
the blue planet.
All the water
makes it look
blue from space.

All living things need water. Plants need water to grow. People and animals need water to live, too.

Scientists have found ice on other planets. But it seems only Earth has the liquid water living things need.

What's inside Earth?

Earth is a rocky planet. It has layers. The centre is hot metal. The outer layers are rock. The surface is called the crust. The crust is always moving, very slowly. It is cracked, like a broken eggshell.

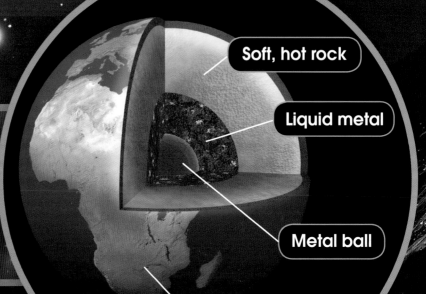

Soft, hot rock

Liquid metal

Metal ball

Rocky crust

The hot metal ball in Earth's centre is called the core. Around it is liquid metal, then layers of rock.

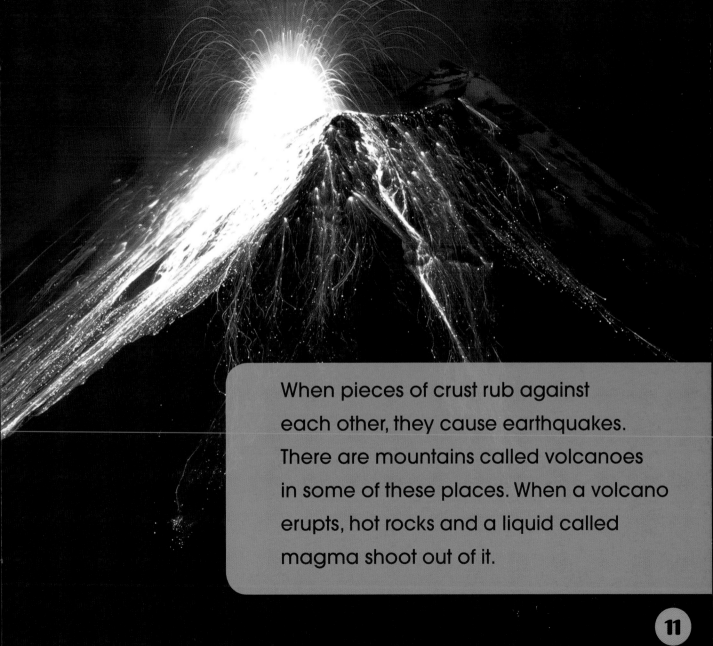

When pieces of crust rub against each other, they cause earthquakes. There are mountains called volcanoes in some of these places. When a volcano erupts, hot rocks and a liquid called magma shoot out of it.

Day and night

The Sun rises and sets because Earth spins around, like a spinning top. When the part of Earth you live on faces the Sun, it is day. When your part of Earth faces away from the Sun, it is night.

Earth takes 24 hours, or one day, to spin all the way around once.

Earth

Sun's rays

Sun

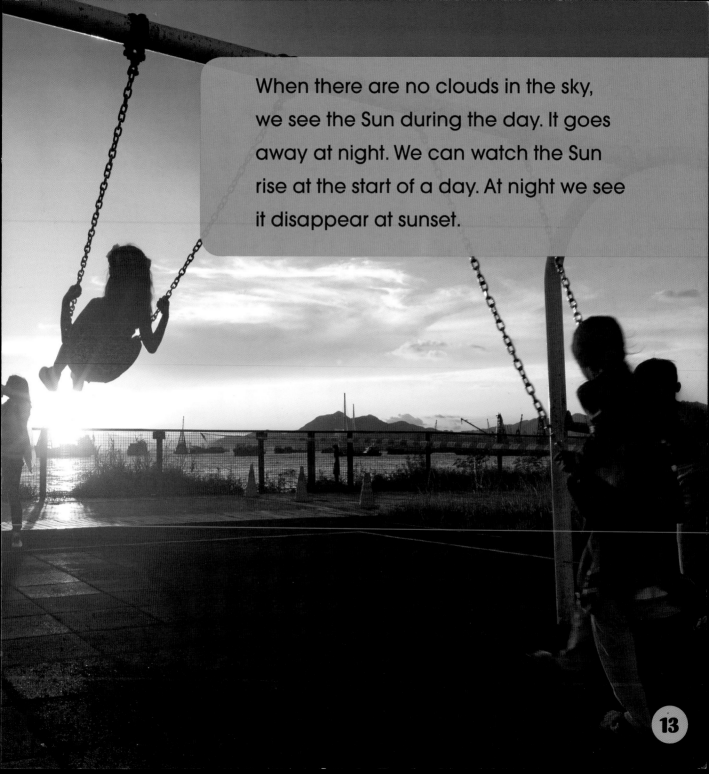

When there are no clouds in the sky, we see the Sun during the day. It goes away at night. We can watch the Sun rise at the start of a day. At night we see it disappear at sunset.

Summer and winter

Earth moves around, or orbits, the Sun. As it moves, Earth tilts, or leans over. The part that tilts towards the Sun is warmer.

Earth takes just over 365 days (a year) to go around the Sun once.

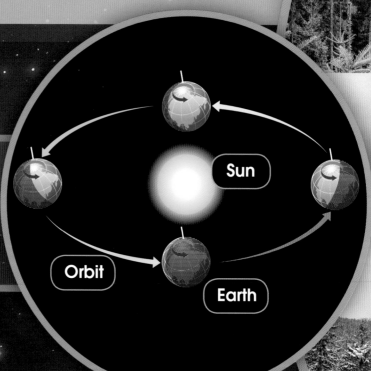

Sun

Orbit

Earth

The part of Earth that tilts towards the Sun has summer. The Sun rises early in the morning and sets late in the day.

Six months later, this part of Earth tilts away from the Sun. Then it is winter there. The Sun rises later and sets earlier.

Earth's weather

The weather on Earth changes from day to day. It can be sunny, cloudy, windy or rainy. It can be hot or cold. Sometimes it snows.

There can be thunder and lightning during a rainstorm.

The weather is hottest near the equator. It is coldest at the North and South Poles.

North Pole

Equator

South Pole

The weather changes from place to place, too. Places near the equator are hottest because they get the most sunshine through the year.

Air moves around the Earth all the time, making wind and changing the weather.

Exploring space

People on Earth want to know more about space. In ancient times, people looked up at the stars. Now scientists send rockets into space. Space probes visit other planets. They send back information and photos to Earth.

The *Cassini* space probe is finding out about the planet Saturn.

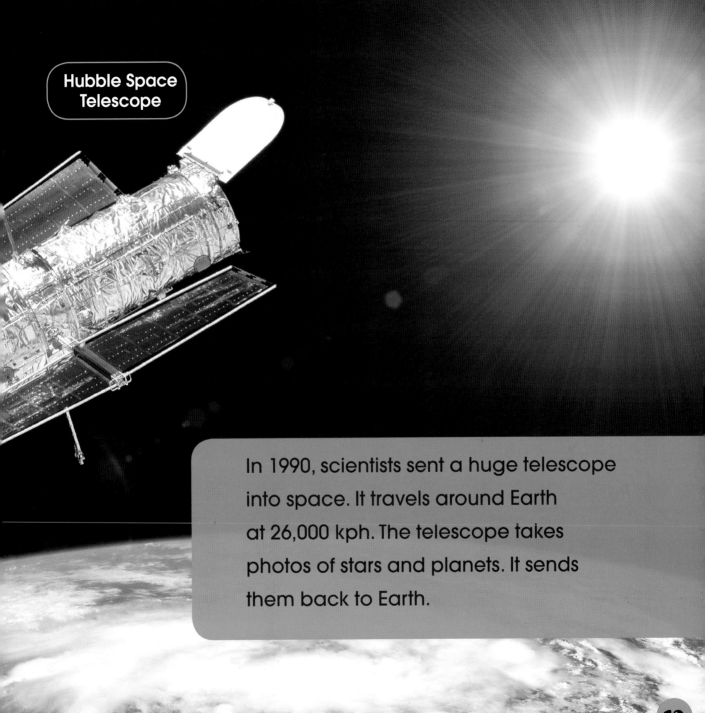

Hubble Space Telescope

In 1990, scientists sent a huge telescope into space. It travels around Earth at 26,000 kph. The telescope takes photos of stars and planets. It sends them back to Earth.

19

Space explorers

A space explorer is called an astronaut. People went into space for the first time in 1961. In 1969 the first people landed on the Moon. Since 2000 astronauts have lived in space on a space station.

Astronauts wear spacesuits when they step into space.

The International Space Station floats 370 km above Earth.

It is called the International Space Station. Astronauts stay there for about six months at a time. They come from different countries. They do experiments while they are on the space station.

Make a model earth

What you need

6 pieces of modelling clay:
   2 small, 2 medium, 2 big

Food colouring
Dental floss

What to do

1. Colour the small clay pieces red and green, the medium pieces orange and brown and the large pieces blue and yellow.

2. Roll the red clay into a ball (this will be the core).

3. Wrap the orange clay around the red ball. Pinch the edges together.

4. Wrap the yellow clay around the orange. Do the same with the brown and then the blue clay.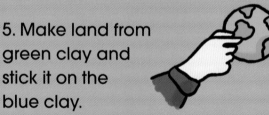

5. Make land from green clay and stick it on the blue clay.

6. Cut your Earth in half with a piece of dental floss.

Useful words

astronaut
Someone who goes
into space on a spacecraft.

atmosphere
The layer of gases around
a planet, moon or star.

equator
The invisible line around
the middle of Earth.

orbit
To move around another
object.

oxygen
An invisible gas in the air.
Living things breathe
oxygen.

planet
A large object in space that
orbits the Sun or another star.

space probe
A spacecraft that does not
have people on board.

Sun
The star at the centre of the
solar system.

Find out more

Websites

www.kidsastronomy.com/earth.htm

www.planetsforkids.org/planet-earth.html

ngkids.co.uk/science-and-nature/universe-facts

Books

Fact Cat Earth, Alice Harman (Wayland, 2015)

First Fabulous Facts Space, Anita Ganeri (Ladybird, 2014)

Solar System (DK Findout!), (DK, 2016)

Index